Student's Book

Unit 6

In Unit 6, children will learn and practise:

- describing what they can see using 'There is… and 'There are…'
- using the present simple in statements and questions
- asking and answering questions about preferences
- providing short positive and negative answers to questions
- using conjunctions to make longer sentences
- using possessive adjectives and other adjectives to describe objects and people
- describing weather conditions and times of the day
- offering and accepting politely
- identifying words and images for shapes, musical instruments and new foods
- recognising the same sounds and letter patterns in words

Unit 6 Contents

Unit 6 Topics

Topic 1 My favourite room

 My favourite room is the living room.

big ★ new ★ nice ★ old small

armchair ★ bookcase clock ★ mat ★ painting radio ★ rug ★ sofa ★ TV wall

behind ★ in ★ next to on ★ under

colours

What can you see?

Match the sentences and pictures.

1 There is a nice painting on the wall. ....5....
2 There is a big, yellow sofa. ....3....
3 My favourite room is the living room. ....1....
4 What can you see in the living room? ....2....
5 There are two blue armchairs. ....4....

 Let's play a game!

Write the word. Look and circle yes or no.

There's a (llyewo) y_e_l_l_o_w sofa.   Yes (No)

There are two (eulb) b_l_u_e armchairs. (Yes) No

There's a (enic) n_i_c_e painting.   (Yes) No

There's a (inkp) p_ _ _ _ rug.   Yes No

There's a (klacb) _ _ _ck TV.   Yes No

There's a (rowbr) b_ _ _ _ _ bookcase.   Yes No

 Let's play a game!

4

 **Read and colour.**

a red armchair	a purple bookcase	a green rug
a blue clock	a brown sofa	an orange door

Write the sentence.

a sofa. brown There's — There's a brown sofa.

red There's armchair. a — ....

rug. a green There's — ....

There's bookcase. a purple — ....

Colour me

Let's play a game!

Put the words in the correct group. Write the word.

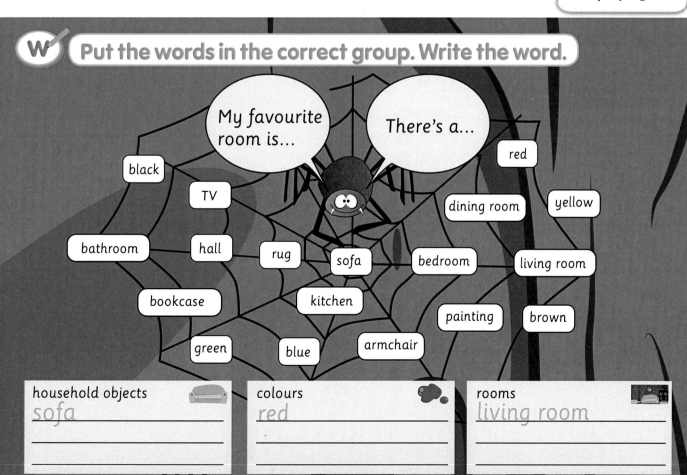

My favourite room is...

There's a...

black

TV

red

dining room

yellow

bathroom   hall   rug   sofa   bedroom   living room

bookcase   kitchen   painting   brown

green   blue   armchair

household objects	colours	rooms
sofa	red	living room
	blue	

5

Match the words to the pictures. Draw a line.

beautiful ⋆ happy
grandmother ⋆ mother
camera ⋆ flowers
a present ⋆ time ⋆ today
get ⋆ give ⋆ have ⋆ cake
have lemonade
have a party
take a photo
say 'thanks a lot'
It's Mothers' day today!

grandmother   beautiful flowers   take a photo

mother   happy   camera

Hit the gong

Let's play a game!

Thanks a lot!

have lemonade   give a present   have cake

 Match the picture and sentence.

My mother says, "Thanks a lot."   Ⓒ

It's Mothers' Day today.   ◯

We give my mother some beautiful flowers and a present.   ◯

 Read the sentences. Write yes or no.

There is a grandmother drinking milk.   ......no......

There is a sad family.

The family is eating burgers.

There is a camera.

There is a cake.

 Write a sentence about the picture.

There is a ....

✓ Write the word. Match the picture and the sentence.

⬭ I **g i v e** my mother a present. (v e i g)

⬭ We give my _ _ _ _ _ _ beautiful flowers. (r o m e h t)

⬭ We _took_e a photo. (k e t a)

⬭ I _have_ lemonade. (v e h a)

⬭ We have _ _ _ _. (e k c a)

⬭ We are _ _ _ _ _. (p a h y p)

Spelling bee

Let's play a game!

🎨 Match the words.

beautiful
have
happy
take

a photo
family
cake
flowers

Comic story

Let's play a game!

✓ Write the words.

 beautiful flowers ....

 ....

 ....

 ....

7

Topic 3 Word building — can you hear the same sounds?

 Match the words and sounds.

mail ★ rain ★ tail ★ train
sail ★ snail
bee ★ feet ★ see ★ sheep
sleep ★ tree

rain

ai

ee

sheep

train

sleep

tail

see

tree

bee

mail

feet

snail

sail

Look at the pictures. Say the words. Circle the odd one out.

Write a word that rhymes.

1 train   <u>rain</u>

2 bee   ....

3 sheep   ....

4 snail   ....

❶

❷

❸

❹

Trivia 2
Let's play a game!

8

Write the letters to complete each word.

ai	ee
m <u>ai</u> l	b <u>ee</u>
r <u>ai</u> n	f <u>ee</u> t
t <u>ai</u> l	s <u>ee</u>
tr <u>ai</u> n	sh <u>ee</u> p
s <u>ai</u> l	sl <u>ee</u> p
sn <u>ai</u> l	tr <u>ee</u>

Let's play a game!

 Write the letters to make a word.

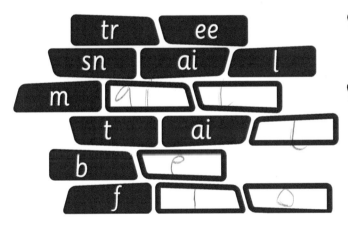

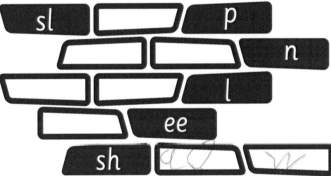

 Look at the pictures. Write the words.

 I like my toy train
I don't like <u>r a i n</u>!

 Can you see the bee
Sitting in the _ __ _ .

 It's time to sleep!
Let's count
_ _ _ _ _!

 Look at the snail!
It's got a big _ __ _ .

Match the words and pictures.

beautiful ⋆ big ⋆ happy
new ⋆ nice ⋆ old ⋆ small
behind ⋆ in ⋆ next to
on ⋆ under
colours
family
household objects
It's my party today.
This is my Mum.

a green sofa   a grey armchair   a blue bookcase

a painting   a black TV

a purple rug   a red clock   a wall   a brown radio

Let's play a game!

 Read and circle the name.

Who likes the living room?	Dan	Grace	father
Who is giving the flowers?	Dan	Grace	father
Who is taking the photo?	Dan	Grace	father

 Put the words in the correct group. Write the word.

grandmother   giving a present   taking a photo

having cake   flowers   mother   camera   cake

Activity

giving a present

h _ _ _ _ _

_ a k _

t _ _ i _ _ _ a

_ h _ t _

Family
grandmother

_ _ _ _ _ er

Party
cake

f _ _ w _ r _

c _ _ _ _ _ a

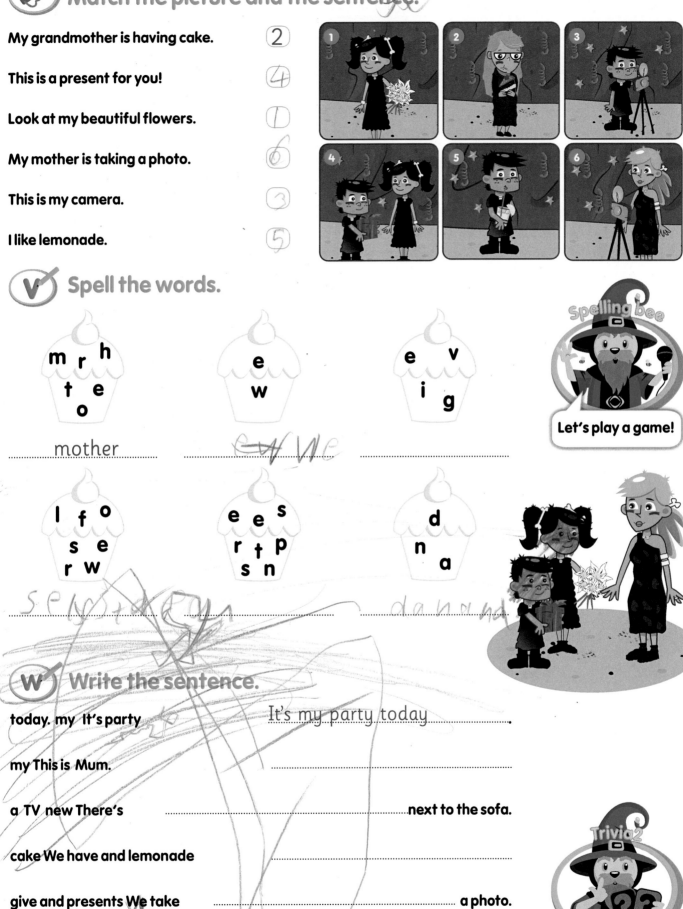

Match the picture and the sentence.

My grandmother is having cake.   ②

This is a present for you!   ④

Look at my beautiful flowers.   ①

My mother is taking a photo.   ⑥

This is my camera.   ③

I like lemonade.   ⑤

Spell the words.

m r h t e o

e w

e v i g

.... mother ....

l f o s e r w

e e s r t p s n

d n a

....

Let's play a game!

Write the sentence.

today. my It's party   It's my party today

my This is Mum.   ....

a TV new There's   .... next to the sofa.

cake We have and lemonade   ....

give and presents We take   .... a photo.

Let's play a game!

11

Draw a line between the words and pictures.

clothes · shop
big · new · small
clothes
colours
I want a new jacket.
It's too big. · It's too small.

clothes shop — jacket — brown — T-shirt — trousers

shoes — too small — too big — orange

Washing line

Let's play a game!

 Circle the correct answer.

Dan wants	(a) a new shirt	(b) a new jacket	(c) new shoes
Dan and his dad go to the	(a) toy shop	(b) party shop	(c) clothes shop
The green jacket is	(a) too small	(b) too big	(c) OK
The yellow jacket is	(a) too small	(b) too big	(c) OK
Dan likes the	(a) orange jacket	(b) blue jacket	(c) green jacket

Read and colour. Write the words.

big green jacket   a small yellow pair of shoes   a big black T-shirt

a big brown hat   **Clothes Shop**   small blue jacket

It's too
_ _ _ _ .

It's too
_ _ _ _ _ _ .

a small orange T-shirt   a big red pair of shoes   a small purple hat

 Write the word.

o p sh

.... shop ....

o s l e c th

....

oo s b t

....

Matching game

Let's play a game!

j t a ck e

....

s ea n j

....

o s ck s

....

 Write the sentence.

want I new some socks.   I want some new socks ....

dress. new want I a   ....

a want new, I T-shirt. white   ....

big. too are These   ....

are small. These too   ....

Cloze

Let's play a game!

13

Match the words and pictures.

toy | basketball | Jill | Bill | doll | teddy bear | football | train | toy shop

 Match the picture and the sentence.

but ★ not

beautiful ★ big ★ great
nice

toys

She doesn't like football but she likes basketball.

The brown teddy bear is nice but the small doll is not.

Jill doesn't like dolls but she likes teddy bears. ○

Bill gets the teddy bear and the basketball. ○

The brown teddy bear is nice but the small doll is not. ○

Bill goes to the toy shop. ○

The black and white football is nice but the orange basketball is great! ○

Jill doesn't like football but she likes basketball. ○

 Write the sentence.

This is a ball

Let's play a game!

Read the sentences. Join the pictures.

Jamal likes footballs but not basketballs.

Jill likes teddy bears but not dolls.

Bill likes trains but not teddy bears.

Hangman

Let's play a game!

 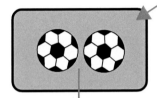 

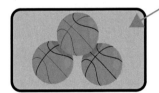  

 Write a sentence about you.

Comic story

Let's play a game!

....

 Look at the pictures. Write the words.

(ball) (Yuki) (nice) (Jill) (Bill) (doll) (beautiful) (Jamal) (big) (train) (great)

....

....

15

✓ What sound do the words start with?

j - jeans ★ jacket ★ jump
v - vegetable ★ violin
w - wave ★ watermelon
y - yellow ★ yo-yo

Trivia2 phonics

Let's play a game!

Match panic

Let's play a game!

✏️ Write the letters in the circles.

j   j   v   v   w   w   y   y

✓ Put the words in the correct group. Write the word.

__acket   __ellow   V̲egetable   __ump   __atermelon

__o-__o   __ave   __iolin

v	w	y	j
vegetable	....	....	....
....	....	....	....

Write sentences.

jumping and like Yuki Jamal waving and

Yuki and Jamal like waving and jumping .

yellow a has jacket Yuki yo-yo a and

....

not likes watermelons but Jamal vegetables

....

Let's play a game!

Finish the words to build the word wall. Put the letters j, v, w or y in the yellow squares.

	j	a		ck	e	t
		a			e	
		o		l		n
	e	ll				
	u	m				
	o			o		
a	e		m	e		o

Match the pictures and words.

a hat — a dress — a skirt — a t-shirt — trousers — socks — jeans — a shirt — a jacket

I want a new T-shirt and some shoes.

I want some socks and a dress.

It's too big!

This hat is beautiful.

a football — shoes — a toy train — a doll — a teddy bear — a ball — a basketball

Do you like the toy train?

Yes, it's great.

I like my new T-shirt, my ball and my nice new shoes!

Yes, I do too!

Circle the correct answer.

but ⋆ not ⋆ play ⋆ shop
some ⋆ too
beautiful ⋆ big ⋆ great
new ⋆ nice
clothes ⋆ colours ⋆ toys
These are too big.
These are too small.

Who wants some new shoes?	Jill	Bill
Who wants a new dress?	Jill	Bill
Who likes the hat?	Jill	Bill
Who likes the toy train?	Jill	Bill

 Read the sentences. Put a tick ✔ or a cross ✗.

Bill and Jill want to go to the food shop. ✗

Bill wants some socks.

Jill wants a dress.

Bill wants a ball.

Bill likes his ball.

Let's play a game!

18

 **Write the words.**

Let's play a game!

toys	clothes
tr_ _n	ja_ _et
b_ _ _	so_ _s
do_ _	_k ir_
_e_ _y _ear	t - _ _irt
f_ _tb_ _ _	_eans
_a_ketb_ _ _	_res_

 Look at the pictures. Write the words in the gaps.

| shoes | train | T-shirt | bananas | dolls | ball | teddy bear |

Bill and Jill go to the clothes shop. He wants a new T-................... She wants some new s................... They go to the toy shop. Jill doesn't like d................... but she likes the b................... Bill likes the t...................

 Write the words in the correct group.

| shirt | train | skirt | orange | trousers | grey | jeans | basketball |

| T-shirt | football | purple | yellow | doll | ball | white |

Picaro's Toy Shop

train

Picaro's Clothes Shop

Picaro's Paint Shop

Read the story.

Mr Brown	trumpet	violin	drums	teacher

teacher

drums ★ guitar ★ music

piano ★ trumpet ★ violin xylophone

her ★ his ★ my ★ our your

play ★ sing

Can you play the guitar?

I can play the guitar but I can't sing.

This is Mr Brown.

He is our music teacher.

This is my guitar.

Can you play the guitar?

I can play the guitar.

but I can't sing!

guitar	piano	xylophone	music	sing

 Match the pictures and words.

Pelmanism

Let's play a game!

Ferris wheel

Let's play a game!

Read the sentences. Put a tick ✓ or a cross ✗.

This is Mr Brown.	✓
Mr Brown is an English teacher.	☐
Yuki has a violin.	☐
Jamal can play the guitar.	☐
Jamal can sing.	☐

Look at the pictures. Write the words.

(his) (my) (our) (your)

I can play
— — guitar.

Can I play
— — — —
guitar, Yuki?

We are
playing — — —
drums!

Charlie loves
to play — — —
drums.

 **Write sentences about you.**

I can
I can't

play
swim
sing

the guitar.
the piano.
the drums.
football.

I can ....

but I can't ....

W **Write the sentences.**

Brown. This Mr is   This is Mr Brown. ....

music He teacher. our is   ....

my guitar. is This   ....

play Can the you guitar?   ....

I can the can't but guitar play I sing.   ....

Let's play a game!

21

Read the story. Match the pictures and words.

first ★ second ★ third
afternoon ★ morning
cloudy ★ hot ★ rainy
sunny
She's first. ★ He's second.

morning sunny hot third second

a It's Sports Day today!

Sports Day

b Morning
It's sunny!
It's hot!

c Afternoon
It's cloudy!
It's rainy!

Matching game
Let's play a game!

d Nick runs very fast!

e I'm first!
I'm third!
I'm second!
Sports Day

cloudy rainy afternoon first fast

Match the picture and the sentence.

He's first. ⟶ e

It's sunny in the morning...

Nick runs very fast.

It's Sports Day today.

...but it's rainy in the afternoon.

Answer the questions. Circle the correct answer.

Is it Sports Day?	yes	no
What is the weather like?	sunny	rainy
Who is running fast?	Yuki	Nick
Who is second?	Yuki	Charlie
How many characters are running?	4	3

Hotspot click

Let's play a game!

 Look at the pictures and words. Complete the sentences.

cats   sun   sports   friends   clouds   Nick   train

It's .... Day today. It's sunny in the morning. I can
see the .... but I can see some .... too.
It's rainy in the afternoon. .... runs very fast.
His .... are happy.

Comic story

Let's play a game!

 Write the words in the correct group.

Yuki   jump   Bill   hot   wear a T-shirt   run   rainy   Charlie

cloudy   Jill   wear shorts   sunny

verbs	weather	names
jump		

Read the poem.

ball ★ small ★ tall ★ wall
hand ★ sand ★ stand
Bill ★ hill ★ Jill ★ pill

This is Jill! This is Bill!
Jill and Bill climb a hill.

Bill is tall. Jill is small.
Jill and Bill bounce a ball.

Bill and Jill hand in hand
Run and play on the sand

Jill and Bill on a wall.
The wall is very tall.

Bill and Jill hold their hands!
Don't jump! Stop and stand.

Bill and Jill feel very ill!
Mr Picaro gives them a pill.

 Read and circle yes or no.

Jill and Bill climb a tree.	yes	no
Jill is tall.	yes	no
Jill and Bill bounce a ball.	yes	no
Bill and Jill feel ill.	yes	no
Mr Picaro gives them an apple.	yes	no

Let's play a game!

Make words. Write them.

b	-all	ball
p		pill
s		sand
sm		
j	-and	
h		
st		
t		
w	-ill	

Hangman

Let's play a game!

 Write the words. What is the sentence?

climb

d a n

....

....

....

....

Match-panic

Let's play a game!

 Circle the odd one out.

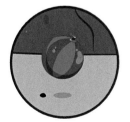

ball
small
pill

tall
wall
Jill

hand
small
sand

stand
Bill
hill

Jill
pill
tall

Complete the words.

teacher
afternoon ★ morning
cloudy ★ hot ★ rainy
sunny ★ weather
drums ★ guitar ★ music
piano ★ trumpet ★ violin
xylophone
her ★ his ★ my ★ our
your
first ★ second ★ third
fast
jump ★ play ★ run ★ sing
wear a T-shirt ★ wear
shorts
He's first. ★ She's second.
Can you run fast?

gui_t_ar   _orning   h_t   thir_   seco_d

Sports Day
Music Day

sports _eacher   Char_ie   _ick   after_oon

_ainy   _ _oudy   _uki

Hit the gong

Let's play a game!

s _ _ _ y   _ill   play _usic   Bi_ _   _irst

 Match the words and pictures.

Answer the questions.

How many teachers are there?	4	2
Who is the sports teacher?	Mr Brown	Mr Green
What is Yuki playing?	the violin	the guitar
What is Jamal doing?	jumping	running
Who is first?	Jamal	Bill

Let's play a game!

Write the picture number next to the sentence.

This is Mr Brown. He's my music teacher. 6

It's a rainy day! ⬭

Can you play the guitar? ⬭

I'm first! ⬭

I can run fast! ⬭

It's Sports Day today! ⬭

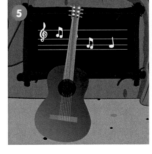

 Make the words.

y t d a o ....

e y r v ....

t i s f r ....

o i v l n i ....

 **Write the words in the story.**

It's Sports Day and Music Day
_ _ _ _ _. Jamal runs
_ _ _ _ _ fast. He's _ _ _ _ _.
Yuki plays the _ _ _ _ _ _.
She's first too.

Let's play a game!

27

✓ Write the word in the box.

(motorbike) (afternoon) (bus) (train) (car) (walk) (morning)

How do you go to school?

train

I go to school on the bus in the morning.

How does Draco go home in the evening?

Draco goes home in his car in the evening.

afternoon ★ evening
morning ★ night
bus ★ car ★ motorbike
train ★ walk
How do you go to school?
I go to school on the bus in the morning.

Circle the correct answer.

How many motorbikes are there?	one	four
Yuki goes to school at 8 in the...?	afternoon	morning
Who goes to school by bus?	Yuki	Mr Picaro
Draco goes home at 3 in the...?	afternoon	evening
Who goes home by car?	Yuki	Draco

Hangman

Let's play a game!

Write the word in the clock.

.....morning..... ....

 Write the words in the story.

(bus) (motorbike) (train) (motorbikes) (car) (horse) (cars)

I go to school by c_a_ _r_. I have three blue toy c_ _ _ at home.

Yuki likes pink _ _ _ _ _ _ _ _ _ _ _.

She goes to school by _ _ _.

Jamal goes to school by _ _ _ _ _. He likes trains.

Hangman Trivia2

Let's play a game!

 Complete the sentences.

How do you go to school?

I go to school ....

How do you go home?

I go home ....

What do you do in the morning?

I .... in the morning.

What do you do in the afternoon?

I .... in the afternoon.

What do you do in the evening?

I .... in the evening.

What do you do at night?

I .... at night.

29

Read and complete the story.

Food
Would you like...?
Yes, please, I'd like...
No, thanks. I'd like...
Here you are.

Would you like .... ?

Yes, please, I'd like ....

No, thanks. I'd like ....

Here you are.

 Write the word in the correct place.

cakes   burger   chips   milk   tomato   chicken   fish

sausages   lemonade   ice-cream

tomato

Pelmanism

Let's play a game!

30

Answer the question with one word.

a) What would Jamal like?   some c h i p s

b) What is Jamal doing?   _ _ _ _ing

c) What's in the picture?   _ _ _ _ _ _ _ _

d) How many sausages are there?   th_ _ _

e) What drink does Jamal have?   _ _ _ _

Complete the sentences.

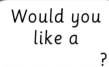 Would you like a _ _ _ _ _?

 Would you like some _ _ _ _ _ _?

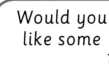 Here you are.

 Yes, please, I'd like a _ _ _ _ _ _.

 Yes, please, I'd like some _ _ _ _ _ _ _ _.

 Thank you!

 chips    lemonade    food   burger    apples

Write the words in the correct place.

ice-cream tomato chips chicken cakes milk fish burger sausages lemonade	I'd like some...	I'd like a(n)...
	....	ice-cream
	....	....
	....	....
	....	....

Write the words. Circle the words that end in -ck or -g.

-ck — black ★ clock ★ duck kick ★ Nick ★ sick ★ sock tick

-g — bag ★ big ★ bug dog ★ frog ★ jug ★ leg pig

Bug has a jug.

It's a big black j u g.

Bug likes his j _ _.

Duck has a bag.

It's a big black b _ _.

D _ _ _ likes her bag.

Pig has a s _ _ _.

It's a big black sock.

Pig likes his s _ _ _.

Dog has a clock.

The c _ _ _ _ goes tick-tock!

D _ _ likes his clock.

Picaroon Nick

Has a ball to k _ _ _.

Nick likes to kick.

Bug, Duck and Nick

And Dog and Pig kick.

They like to kick!

Sound maze
Let's play a game!

Hangman
Let's play a game!

Make a Word
Let's play a game!

Match the words to a picture.

Make and write some words.

Nick

....

....

....

....

....

....

N
j
bl
b
cl
d
s
fr

a
e
i
o
u

ck
g

Complete the sentences.

I like frogs but I don't like dogs.

I have some socks but I don't have a jug.

I want a clock but I don't want a bag.

I like .... but I don't like ....

I have ....

.... but I don't have ....

I want .... but I don't want ....

Write the words in the correct place.

-ck	-g
	jug

bla__   ju g   le__

si__   pi__   Ni__

bu__   so__   ba__

ki__   clo__   du__

fro__   ti__   bi__

do__

33

How do you go to the café?

food

afternoon ★ evening
morning ★ night

bus ★ car ★ motorbike
train ★ walk

How do you go to the café?

Matching game

Let's play a game!

 Read the sentences. Put a tick ✔ or a cross ✘ in the box

Zoe walks to the café in the morning.	✔
Draco goes to the café by motorbike in the morning.	☐
Charlie goes to the café by train in the morning.	☐
Jamal goes to the café by motorbike in the evening.	☐
Yuki goes to the café by car at night.	☐

 Write the words in the correct place.

s<u>a u s a g e s</u>, ch_ _ _ _   ch_ _ _ _ _, ch_ _ _ _

and _ _ _ _   and i_ _ _ _ ea_

b_ _ _ _ _ _, t_ _ _ o   _ _ _ _ and _ _ _ _ _

and _ _ _ _ _ _ _ _ _   and _ ake

Complete the dialogue and the picture.

Odd one out
Let's play a game!

Match panic
Let's play a game!

No, thanks. I'd like _____ .

Would you like _____ ?

Here you are.

Yes, please, I'd like _____ .

 Write the words in the sentences.

dining room | a burger | bread | afternoon | kitchen | milk | café

morning | chicken | evening

I go to the _____kitchen_____ in the m___orning_____

to eat _____bread_____ and drink _____milk_____ .

I go to the _____ in the a_____

to eat _____ .

I go to the _____ in the e_____

to eat _____ .

✔ **Write the word next to the shape.**

circle ★ line ★ oval
rectangle ★ square ★ star
triangle
What shape is the apple?
The apple is a circle.

(triangle) (line) (oval) (star) (square) (circle) (rectangle)

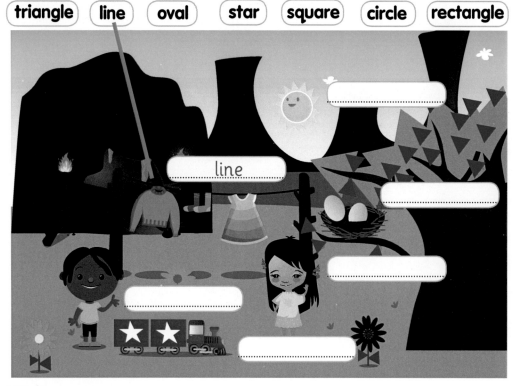

line

📖 **Write yes or no.**

The sun is a circle. .... yes ....

The clothes are on a line. ....

The train is a triangle. ....

There's a star on the train. ....

The leaves are rectangles. ....

Pelmanism

Let's play a game!

✔ **Write the words. Match it to a picture.**

triangle.................. ....

Circle the correct answer.

Where are the tomatoes?	In the circle	In the square
Where's the bus?	In the star	In the rectangle
Where's the violin?	In the square	In the triangle
Where are the Picaroons?	In the star	In the circle

 Answer the questions.

Find the green triangle. How many are there? ....

Find the red circles. How many are there? ....

Find the rectangles. What colour are they? ....

What is Draco doing? ....

Find the squares. What colour are they? ....

Picture drag
Hotspot click

Let's play a game!

 Draw a picture above the word.

triangle   oval   square   rectangle

line   star   circle

37

Draw a line between the words and pictures.

(white star) (nose) (body) (yellow circle) (funny) (blue oval)

(red rectangle) (green legs) (black triangle)

angry ★ beautiful ★ funny
short ★ tall ★ ugly
body
colours
shapes
What does your monster look like?
My monster is beautiful.

What does your monster look like?

My monster is beautiful. He has a big red nose.

Pelmanism

Let's play a game!

My monster has a big square head, a funny body and green legs.

He has 3 eyes and 2 noses!

Read and circle.

Who has a monster with green legs?	Jamal	Yuki
Who has a monster with a red nose?	Jamal	Yuki
Who has a beautiful monster?	Jamal	Yuki
Who has a monster with a funny body?	Jamal	Yuki

Trivia2
Colour me

Let's play a game!

Complete the sentences. Write yes or no.

There is a white s t a r on the table. ....

Jamal's monster is __ eau __ i __ __ __ __ ....

Yuki's monster has a small __ ea __ . ...

Jamal's monster has a big __ __ __ e ....

Draw a line between the monsters and the correct sentence.

This monster is funny. **This monster is angry.** **This monster is ugly.**

Read, draw and colour the monster.

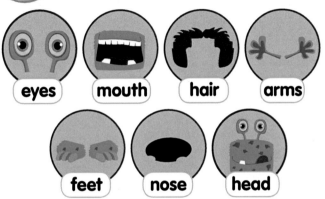

eyes   mouth   hair   arms

feet   nose   head

The monster has a big oval head, an ugly body and short legs. It has four angry eyes and two blue noses. Its arms and legs are green. Its body is brown.

My monster ....

 Write the words in the correct place.

ugly   tall   beautiful   funny   arms   face   star   circle   angry

triangle   short   eyes   head   hand   oval   legs   square   rectangle

adjectives	body	shapes
beautiful	eyes	triangle

Write the words in the correct place.

Words, sounds and letters from Unit 6

Mr Snail likes to s a i l,

Mr Dog has a _ _ _ _,

Mr Duck has a _ _ _ _ _

And Mr Pig is _ _ _.

Mr Bee's in a _ _ _ _,

Picaroon Nick is _ _ _ _,

Mr Sheep has four _ _ _ _

And Mr Wall is _ _ _ _.

Picaroon Bill is _ _ _ ,

Mr Small has a _ _ _ _,

Mr Sock has a _ _ _ _ _

And Mr Hand likes _ _ _ _.

Mr Bug has a _ _ _,

Picaroon Jill likes _ _ _ _ _ _ s,

Mr Mail has a _ _ _ _

And Mr Train likes _ _ _ _.

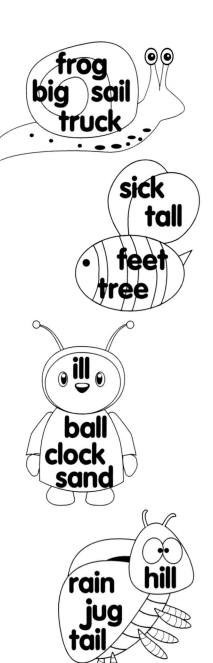

frog
big sail
truck

sick
tall
feet
tree

ill
ball
clock
sand

rain hill
jug
tail

  Put a tick ✔ or a cross ✗ next to the sentence.

Odd one out

Let's play a game!

 starts with 'v'. ✔

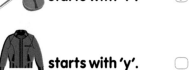 starts with 'y'. ☐

starts with 'y'. ☐

starts with 'w'. ☐

starts with 'j'. ☐

starts with 'v'. ☐

starts with 'j'. ☐

 starts with 'w'. ☐

Duck Arcade

Let's play a game!

Write some sentences that rhyme.

I like <u>s h e e p</u> (eehps)

And I like to _ _ _ _ _ (eespl) !

I like _ _ _ _ _ (sksco)

And I like _ _ _ _ _ _ _ (occkls)

I like ....

And I like ....

I like bees and I like trees!

 Draw a line between words sound pairs.

 leg

 sleep

 violin

 kick

 tree

 black

 bag

 vegetables

Submarine game

Let's play a game!

Draw a line between the pictures and the letter-sounds.

| y | -ill | j | -all | v | -ck | w | ee | ai | and | -g |

Un-jumble the letters to make words.

 Write the missing letters to complete the words.

.... jacket ....

Clothes
Do you like this?
Would you like some sausages?
Find the red square.
Home
Family

....

....

....

....

....

Hit the gong

Let's play a game!

(a) clothes shop	(e) toy shop	(i) sofa	(m) morning
(b) socks	(f) yo-yo	(j) painting	(n) mother
(c) hat	(g) monster	(k) flowers	(o) grandmother
(d) dress	(h) armchair	(l) a present	

Hangman

Let's play a game!

....

....

....

Cloze

Let's play a game!

....

....

....

(p) music	(t) sing	(x) cakes	(2) square	(6) night
(q) guitar	(u) burger	(y) tomato	(3) circle	(7) motorbike
(r) xylophone	(v) chicken	(z) afternoon	(4) oval	(8) monster
(s) trumpet	(w) sausages	(1) rainy	(5) rectangle	

UNIVERSITY *of* CAMBRIDGE
ESOL Examinations

KAPLAN INTERNATIONAL
COLLEGES

Baby*tv* A FOX
INTERNATIONAL
CHANNEL

ISBN 978-1-909318-15-1

9 781909 318151